I0099534

# ANOTHER DAWN

# ANOTHER DAWN

Poems by
Esther M. Huhn

Another Dawn

Copyright © 2025 Esther M. Huhn

ISBN 979-8-9899529-1-5 (print)

Scripture quotations taken from The Holy Bible, New International
Version®, NIV®. Copyright © 1973, 1978, 1984, 2011 by Biblica, Inc.
Used with permission of Zondervan. All rights reserved worldwide. www.
zondervan.com


Cover illustration © 2025 by Esther McRae. Used by permission.
Cover design and interior layout by Callie Johnson.
Interior illustrations © 2025 by artists:
Kia Hunt, pp. 20, 64;
Callie Johnson, p. 24;
Maddie Huisman, pp. 4, 70.
Used by permission.

All rights reserved.

Published by Cornerstone Art and Craft Collaborative, LLC
Overland Park, Kansas

cornerstone-collaborative.com

For you,
the reader

*I run in the path of your commands,*
*for you have broadened my understanding.*
—Psalm 119:32

# CONTENTS

# ON BECOMING AWARE
*a preface*

Peace arrives peacefully,
as well as love and goodness
and faithfulness. These are manifest
around us without our awareness.
Yet our hearts ache within us
because we live unaware.

Breathe in unison with God.
Comprehend his nearness.
Be silent. Be audible.
Be available.
Call him Father.

When frustration and confusion
and worry and fear and lies
begin to slip away unnoticed,
and *Presence* takes their place,
give thanks.

Practicing a new posture
may take some time, but
you will not miss the bombardment
of thoughts and actions
holding you unaware—

you will simply perceive
these have gone. And when they return,
you will find courage flowing
within awareness.

## ANOTHER DAWN

At sunrise, I lifted pen
to a blank page.
Words refused to form.
They dissolved,
separated into letters, then threw
themselves adrift— confetti on a sea.
Red flags lined the shore.

Desire pressed confusion
to fill the empty page.
Should I coerce words
to make sense
against their will,
or release twenty-six letters
onto whitecaps?

Erosion slips under my feet.
I roam the shore
to gather tattered pieces.
Saltwater runs through my hands.
I await a poem heaven composes.

Today, or maybe
another dawn.

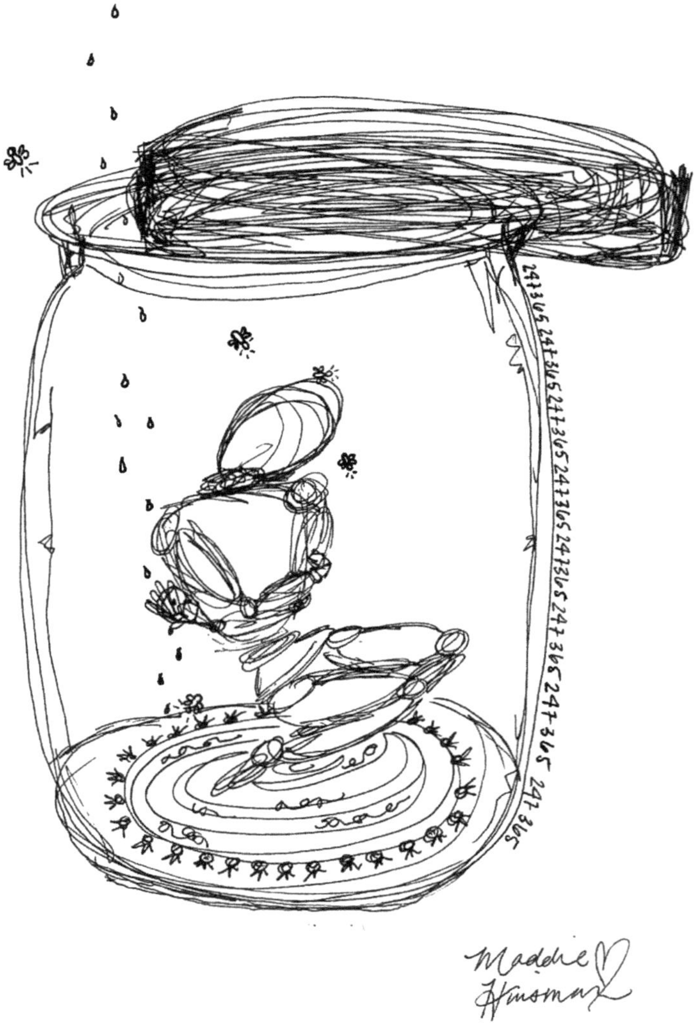
Maddie Hinsman

## MY PSALM

O my soul, why do you concur with hurry?
Output has raised an empire against you.
Emissaries come. Rainfall speaks promise,
lilies whisper gladness, but you rush ahead.

Why does it trouble you to slow down,
match pace with a serene shower, open
your hands, suffer the drops as if you could
catch them and collect them like fireflies?

Lord, the lid is tight on this jar. My soul safe,
detained, I am afraid to be set free.
Help me loose into the evening sky
one messenger of your masterpiece.

O God, please be enough.

# BUILT IN

You will run spent
if you refuse
the deed you know
you ought to do.
Do not deceive
yourself and say
you do not know,
for it was built
inside your heart
long, long ago.

*He has also set eternity in the human heart; yet no one
can fathom what God has done from beginning to end.*

—Ecclesiastes 3:11

# TARGET PRACTICE

First heart
then brain,
unguarded.
Bull's eye.
Dead center.

Integrity collapses
without interruption.
Ghost-like.
Bloodless.

No time to notice,
forge ahead.
Preserve appearance.
No big deal.
Disregard.
Dismiss.

Target riddled.
Lie smirks and pulls the bowstring.

*Take up the shield of faith, with which you can*
*extinguish all the flaming arrows of the evil one.*
—Ephesians 6:16

## MOVING MOUNTAINS

Mountains are moving—
we cannot see.

Maybe the truth is
the mountain to be moved

is me.

## A WISE RELATIONSHIP

Wisdom abides in my heart through trust,
I rest in her heart besides.

Wisdom believes I can be discerning,
I trust in her to be wise.

*Wisdom reposes in the heart of the discerning.*
—Proverbs 14:33

# BRING ME BACK

to the feast of ordinary,
where sparrows banter
across the porch,
sunbeams sneak
between oak branches,
wind rustles
among leaves,
and runoff from rain conducts
the drip, drip, drip
beneath a row of shingles,
keeping the tempo
adagio.

# BEFORE THE NEED FOR TIME

You woke me before
you woke the birds,
to come with you.

You lit my eyes before
you lit the horizon,
to talk to you.

I came where quiet
is an unstirred lake, a child
asleep, a seed in the ground,

an invitation
into awareness—
before the need for time,

before the need for time.


*Be still before the LORD
and wait patiently for him.*

—Psalm 37:7

# IN UNISON

Fog remains. It lingers,
slow to yield its shape,
holding onto unspoken dialogue
between the lover and the beloved
before it fades.

Words invisible. Breath moves
without voice through the lungs,
appearing as a mist on the glass
of a cold window.

Prayer given,
then given back,
breathing
in unison.

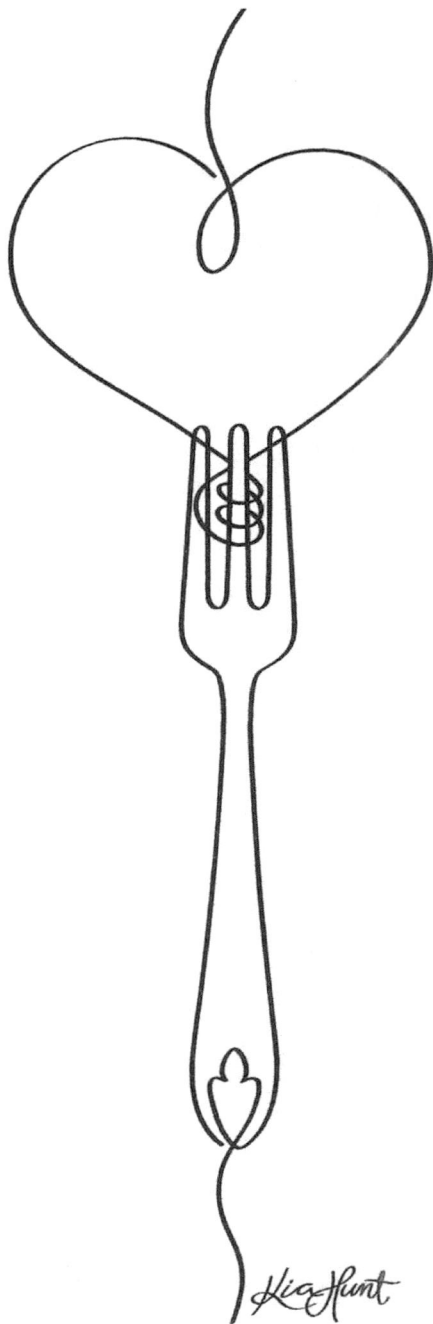

# PRAYER BREAKFAST

Abba Father,

help me sit with you this morning,
not dwelling on the past,
or worried about the future,
but present and content
with love
as the main course.

Help me taste these eggs,
this toast,
this coffee,
and later this afternoon, remember
having received them
and known your pleasure
in them.

Amen.

## ON A DAY LIKE TODAY

Write a few words by sunlight.
Let passing clouds decide
how much light you receive.
Sweep your floors with a broom.
Use the bristles to whisk
away dust particles.

Deadhead your petunias
with a snip of scissors.
Request new blooms.
Wash the window
above the kitchen sink.
Use the yellow rag.

Look through the window,
instead of at the window.

Callie Johnson

# PERFECT TIMING

I pulled my car into our driveway. Today
the black-eyed Susans along our sidewalk
looked like a group of giggling girls
greeting me with a surprise.

One stem bowed like a diva
enjoying her curtain call.
As she sprung back
her top bloom flung upward,

and released a goldfinch.
The Susans stood grand
with all blooms intact
as if nothing had happened.

I am glad I was on time.

# STARS

Tonight, I can count
six, seven, eight,
wait—
ten stars!

I cannot see any others.

That must be all there is.

# WHEN YOU ARE NOT CERTAIN WHAT TO DO

invest some time to examine your shoe,
created to give you support each day.
Look at the style and the way it was made:

each piece cut exactly to the right size,
laces and straps to attract you to buy.
Imagine the worker who took good care
to put it together, ready to wear.

Envision their life and what you would say
if you could meet at their favorite café.
Decide to thank them for all they have done:
"Getting to know you sure has been fun."

Invest some time to examine your shoe
when you are not certain what to do.
And while you are there, support them in prayer.
Consider then, they may have prayed for you.

# ONE STAR IN A DARKENING SKY

Where is the mourning dove? When will it coo?
I crave the lilt in its song, the sway
of three dropped notes, the pause.
A call in my left ear, an answer in my right.
But now, a doleful cry climbs
over the walls into this palace
from my people, my closest kin.
They call. They answer. Do they clamor for me?

I cannot grasp the sackcloth and ashes
of your mourning. I sent you a change of clothes,
an open invitation. Why did you refuse?
Sorrow has swathed me. Our grief
cannot be seen. Mourning may not proceed
through these gates. I have found a home
in this place I did not petition to go.
I remain unseen. Let me linger
where I am sheltered, content
with the echo of mourning doves.

My heart and head
have settled their differences.
Silence arrives as a companion
to your unwelcome news, and places
its hand over the mouth of distress.
I am one star in a darkening sky,
a single reflection
of a promise.

*When Esther's eunuchs and female attendants came and told her*
*about Mordecai, she was in great distress. She sent clothes for*
*him to put on instead of sackcloth, but he would not accept them.*
—Esther 4:4

# BETWEEN LIGHTNING AND THUNDER

*How faint the whisper we hear of him!*
*Who then can understand the thunder of his power?*
—Job 26:14

We expect thunder
to arrive one finger snap
after lightning.

One thousand one,
one thousand two,
one thousand three.

More happens
in the time between
than we can know.

# TUNNEL

She always saw the tunnel,
but the light at the end evaded her.
A handheld flashlight led the way.
Her purpose was to remove flaws,
defects, errors, and stains.
Light would have to appear once
the tunnel was clean.
Day after day she returned
to the hunt. Darkness offered
only darkness. Her flashlight left her stranded.

Despair chipped away
at resolve. Weariness drained
all reserves. She took a chance
that Help remained in the tunnel with her.
"Please God, help me! Is there any good
to be seen here? Is my vision inadequate?
Should I find a better flashlight?

*Click.* Her eyes adjusted. A warm welcome
glowed like a thousand candles. A table
was set for her. The tunnel receded.
She heard a crash as the flashlight fell
from her hand.

> *The light shines in the darkness,*
> *and the darkness has not overcome it.*
>
> —John 1:5

# LIFE ALWAYS PLANNED

holds us hostage.

# NOTEWORTHY

The last thing I want,
Jesus,
is to box you out,
gut you with my elbows,
hush you with pursed lips.

Yet crucifying you
is what I end up doing
to guarantee myself
as somebody
noteworthy.

O, TEARS—


extinguish the fire of my sin.
Hear its flames hiss at your first drop,
watch them wane as you pour out.

Be not dammed, my river of tears,
find mercy as you flow.
Come in great streams,

do not slow until defiance
is drowned. Do not dry
until I concede to the truth of me:

I am a sinner,
            summoned

                        to repentance.

Fall forward and soak the seeds of pardon.
Burst from this body of reserve,
overflow from this urn

of regret, empty the depths of this pool
of disbelief. Come suddenly,
come steadily, come torrentially.

O tears, fall—
slip, spill,
tumble.

# FORSAKEN

*My God, my God, why have you forsaken me?*
—Psalm 22:1; Mark 15:34

Your body seared with the pain
of muscles tearing. Hope drained
with your blood. Those you loved,
you released into grief.

Agony consumed thought.
Doubt ravaged faith. You willed yourself
to greater love. How?
Did you await rescue
from our Father—the One
who sent a ram to replace Isaac?
The God who promised never to forsake
those he loves. Did you wonder,
as I do?

Surrounded by people, I have no one
to hear my story. I wrestle an invisible
partner. I am pinned to the mat.
Condemned if I speak. I shiver,
but cannot come near your fire.
Where is Father?

Your body could no longer resist.
The question burning in your mind
demanded freedom.
You spoke so I could know.

Renounced.
Abandoned.
Alone.
Forsaken.

# REDUCE

my will, Lord,

to liquid,

then pour it out

upon my grave.

# BLANK

is not empty.

# NOT MY HOME

In a world of summer,
I am winter.
In a world of morning,
I am evening.
In a world of day,
I am night.
In a world of dawn,
I am dusk.

## AT SOME POINT

At some point in every day
we lose the truth,
we lose the way.
Not lost in the sense
of forgotten,
but lost in the sense
of forgetting.

## MERCY

Before there was sin there was blessing.

It's evening and I walk burdened. Beneath
a cedar I begin to pray: *Lord Jesus,*
*Son of God, have mercy on me,*
*a sinner.*

*Whoosh, cuta-cuta-cuta-cuta-cuta.*
A swarm of common grackles tears
past me. Prodded by prayer,
the tree has shaken free its residents.

The birds sweep by, bearing
forgiveness with their wings,
and soar toward the sunset sky,
taking my weight with them.

When I dare to unclose my eyes,
clouds bow aside to reveal
the moon— a witness to
the kinship of God
I cannot see.

# I HANG UPON YOUR WORD

for you alone my heart has stirred.
I search for mortal words to mutter,
struggle for what to say. Your Word
pervades what I stumble to utter
on any given day.

To you I will return.

All fleeting speech leaves me wanting.
Every soul strives to say something,
but I hang upon your word,
for you alone my heart has stirred.

And there I will stay.

*If you hold to my teaching, you are really my disciples.*
—John 8:31

# TO REMIND MYSELF

Maple, oak, sweetgum,
birch, and elm become red, russet,
orange, yellow, and burgundy.
Leaves turn and say goodbye
to the tree of their childhood.
Each must go alone and commit
to the ground where thousands
have gone before.

Poetry sings within leaf rain
in their descent of open parachutes
and aerial grace. I bend down and pick up
a leaf fallen from a maple and put it
in my pocket. Crimson burns its way
into my heart.

At home I pause before I remove
this treasure from its shelter. I lay
the red leaf on top of the white counter
to remind myself, when I need to know,
of you and us
and no farewell.

# DISCIPLINE OF SILENCE

Yesterday earth refrained
from movement. It chose
to remain quiet—
no bird ballad,
no leaf shimmer,
no footfall.
Wind abstained
its next breath.

During the night
three inches of rain
arrived in reply
to this discipline
of silence.

*All the earth bows down to you.*

—Psalm 66:4

# WINTER ROBIN

Winter robin sings a song
as if it's a fine spring day.
Winter robin must be wrong,
it's February, not May.

Temperature now is two below;
his flutelike melody charms.
Robin arose and carried on
as if he did not know.

Full-throated notes warm his nest
(winter cannot restrain his song).
Even when times are less than best,
his voice stays clear and strong.

His serenades sail past and ping
from branch to streetlamp to ear;
Robin's song was made to ring
for anyone willing to hear.

# THE GATE

Two decades of time spent
in the sunroom of our home, I never saw
through the backyard gate, which led
to the neighbor's front yard.
The gate was always closed.
Today it was open.
A hint of a whisper told me to look
through to the other side
and see things familiar—
grass, trees, bushes,
people walking their dogs.
I followed this vision
as if I walked upon air.
Beyond the gate, life appeared safe,
secure and welcoming. I wanted
to go through and come back,
go through and come back.
What waited for me there was good.
What held me here was good.
Someone had opened the gate
to show me there is nothing to fear
on either side.

*I am the gate.*

—John 10:9

# MOONSET

This morning, Moon seemed to wait
as I stepped through the backyard gate.
The path turning right I usually take,

but I looked left and held my breath,
I knew Moon would leave too soon.
Both feet replied to my summons to fly—

I am going to touch the moon.
First orange, then yellow, then blue and pink,
Moon dropped faster than I could think.

Was this a game of hide-and-seek
among the houses on my street?
Must Moon retreat for Sun to rise?

With one last wink of moon-man eyes,
Moon was gone at break of dawn.

# MAY I HAVE YOUR ATTENTION PLEASE

Who painted the sycamore white?
Who stood it in front of a sapphire sky?

Way to go—
you made my day!

## WE'VE BEEN GIVEN AN EXTENSION OF TIME

Abba, Father,
we have
an entire hour
together!

Yes, my child,
we have
forever
together.

maddie thurman

# CLOSER THAN WE CAN IMAGINE

*Praise the LORD, my soul;*
*all my inmost being, praise his holy name.*

—Psalm 103:1

After a blessing was prayed to God,
at four o'clock on an ordinary day,
an answer was not expected.
To my mind's eye came a burst
of rose petals leaving my hands
ascending into a world unseen.
I watched them go—however,

before I could think to move on
a shower of red and pink descended
like ribbons encircling me.
In this garden I filled my arms
with petals of love
and tossed them upward.

Grace thrives in blessing.
Blessing thrives in grace.
Both are closer
than we can imagine.

Thank you to everyone for your contribution to this book of devotional poetry. It would not exist without your help:

Christie Ross
Linda Hakes
Kelli Sallman
Barry Huhn
Jonathan Huhn
Members of Write Now

And many others who encouraged me and kept me writing!

This collection has been greatly enhanced by the stunning visual art of:

Kia Hunt
Callie Johnson
Esther McRae
Maddie Huisman

You made this a lot of fun! My deepest gratitude for your creative collaboration.

Thank you, Jesus Christ—my Savior, Friend, and King.
You are the lifter of my head,
the leveler of my ground,
the holder of my tears.
To you be the glory forever.

This is **ESTHER HUHN**'s third book of devotional poetry. She began writing as she entered the empty nest season. Her first book, *Open Hands*, was published in 2022 and is a gift to anyone who would like to request one. Her second book, *Every Day*, was published in 2024 and is available at LuLu Press Bookstore. She continues her lifelong love of walking and enjoying the beauty of God in creation. She also enjoys studio time in her home in Overland Park, Kansas, where she studies and writes poetry.

www.ingramcontent.com/pod-product-compliance
Lightning Source LLC
Chambersburg PA
CBHW062023040426
42447CB00010B/2112